HYPOTHERMIA

HYPOTHERMIA

by Vanessa Brooks

JOSEF WEINBERGER PLAYS

LONDON

HYPOTHERMIA
First published in 2010
by Josef Weinberger Ltd
12-14 Mortimer Street
London W1T 3JJ
www.josef-weinberger.com
general.info@jwmail.co.uk

ISBN: 978 0 85676 322 9

Printed by Commercial Colour Press plc, Hainault, Essex

This play is dedicated to

Ben Langford

A brilliant actor

Thanks to:

FB&TV co-director Lynda Hornsby, Chair David Smith, Vice Chair Mike Smith and all trustees, actors and everyone connected with the first production, publisher Michael Callahan, as ever Mim, and, of course, Mum.

HYPOTHERMIA was first produced by Full Body and the Voice in the round at the Lawrence Batley Theatre, Huddersfield on February 3rd 2010. The cast was as follows:

Oskar	Ben Langford
Dr Erich	Bradley Cole
Lisa	Faye Billing
Dr Katscher	Johnny Vivash
Frau Poppendick	Margaret Fraser

Directed by Vanessa Brooks
Designed by Kevin Jenkins
Lighting Designed by Keith Forryan
Composition and Musical Direction by Laurence Kaye

In the subsequent National UK Tour of *Hypothermia* the role of Oskar was played by James Munton and the role of Dr Erich by Daniel Hoffman-Gill.

April 1940.

Near Andernach. Nazi Germany.

The action takes place in the front office of the State Hospital for hereditary and incurable mental diseases and also on the surface of the frozen lake outside.

Although characters and some locations are fictitious all events are based on historical fact.

Author's Foreword

Full Body and The Voice (FB&TV) is a producing theatre company based in the Lawrence Batley theatre in Huddersfield. In 2004 I answered an advert for writers interested in the company's ongoing exploration of the use of text with actors with learning disabilities. This was left-field and interesting to me. I had one of the most formative and influential periods of my working life during that short project and both my personal perceptions and working processes were changed forever.

Hypothermia sprung partly out of my raised consciousness of the abilities of learning disabled actors, facilitated by the above project, and also due to a long, homesick and contemplative trip to the hottest of places, Australia, in 2006. My cousins Ross and David showed me the best of that extraordinary country, as did the very fondly remembered Auntie Doris and Uncle Alf; but the indolence of my long hot trip threw me into a hunger for work.

By chance I watched a documentary about the Nazis 'T4' project (Tiergarten 4, the Berlin address from which the euthanasia programme was directed). I hadn't been aware of the extent of the Nazi's macabre 'dress rehearsal' for the genocide of the Jewish people, perpetrated on people with disabilities. The Internet contains much documentation of events at the 'killing centres' such as the 'Hadamar Institute' which looms large in *Hypothermia*; hospitals where lethal injections and ultimately lethal gasses were administered to disabled patients. Events and places in *Hypothermia* are based on fact; only the characters are works of fiction though I was, and continue to be, fascinated by people's ability to 'carry on' to 'go the movies and drink schnapps', as Erich says, in the face and knowledge of such callous and industrialised murder.

I began to consider writing a drama with a learning disabled actor at its centre about the most potent of topics; the value of human life and the human capacity for cruelty.

Subsequent to the first draft of *Hypothermia* I sought funding to develop the script and mount a production. I was unaware prior to doing this just how political an arena I was writing into. I was urged to communicate with a leading and much respected writer/ director from the disabled theatre community, and a general intimation through this and other interactions was that a play about the learning disabled genocide by the Nazis should be written only by someone who is themselves disabled. Another intimation from various quarters was that learning disabled people lacked a cogent awareness of the implications of the Nazi genocide and should therefore not be prime movers (actors) in dramas about it and that other agencies working within a specific specialised theatre sector (rather than the notional 'mainstream') were best placed to tell these stories.

I let the play lie for a while as the political machinations and sensitivities surrounding its concept were more arduous than its writing. I directed more. *Hypothermia* however, unlike me, didn't leave with a handkerchief tied to a pole to become a director and with the suspicion that there was a play here worth exploring I put a rehearsed reading together at the Writers Guild centre, then based at Kings Cross. It had too many words in it, Katscher was over-enervated and stereotypical, relationships were undefined and the whole text was peppered with unnecessary 'fucks' – cruelty doesn't need exclamation marks or profanity. Dr Theo Stark, a young doctor and suspected homosexual, was a key protagonist as was Nurse Clara who, during that draft, came in to break the news about the killing of the patients at the Hadamar Institute. In Theo's case his homosexuality was an issue too far, this was a play about disability, and in Clara's case she was off stage too much to warrant the cast size (pragmatics). Both characters needed to be excised and their plot burdens collapsed into other roles. Dr Erich worked alright. Lisa did good enough 'holding it all together' but she needed more of Clara in the mix to make her compelling. As for Oskar? There was the rub . . .

I felt unease watching the non-learning disabled actor who played the role in the reading. He did a fine job but was intrinsically the wrong casting. I had tried without luck to find a learning disabled actor for the reading (there was nowhere to go and, even now, finding an actor with Down's Syndrome in London who could rehearse and deliver a character in the space of an afternoon, is an impossibility).

Time passed and other projects and productions came to the fore. Eventually I took up post as Artistic Director of Full Body and the Voice, where I remain, and programmed *Hypothermia*.

The play was re-written. The cast size was reduced to five (Dr Theo and Clara were cut) and I could now craft the central role of Oskar around the extraordinary Ben Langford*, FB&TV core company actor. An inspirational score was composed by Laurence Kaye and Kevin Jenkins devised an exceptional design for this production in the round. The pilot tour, playing the Lawrence Batley Theatre and Stephen Joseph Theatre, was very well received and it is with confidence that at the time of writing FB&TV prepares for a national tour of the production.

Much as I would love to, this isn't the context in which to break down the processes and methodologies that have allowed a learning disabled actor to take his long overdue place centre stage in a text-based play which reaches mainstream audiences. A further book is planned in the not too distant future which will shine a light on this unique approach and hopefully open the door for many other learning disabled actors to take the place they deserve on major stages – and provide other writers and directors with the means to make the leap into twenty first century theatre.

At the time of going to print, Ben Langford has had to relinquish his role of Oskar in the National Tour due to a mild-but-aggravating illness. He is however happy to pass the baton on to another highly talented FB&TV actor, James Munton, who takes on what has to be one of the best roles around for an actor with a learning disability.

CHARACTERS

DR ERICH   30s–40s. Director of the Hospital. Barely in
                  control. A shaky grip. An atrophied heart.

OSKAR   20s–30s. Learning disabled. Long term
                  patient in the hospital. An observer.
                  Sensitive. Warm.

LISA   29. Administrator. Capable and measured. A
                  paralysed smile.

DR KATSCHER   30s–40s. Charming and athletic. Member of
                  the SS and Reich's committee for the scien
                  tific registration of severe hereditary
                  ailments. A mesmeric blade.

FRAU POPPENDICK   40s–50s. Political zealot. Section Leader of
                  the League of Nazi Women. A fragile icicle.

ACT ONE

Scene One

The frozen lake.

A biting wind grips OSKAR *as he tests the snow with his hands. He checks its consistency. He moves OS left and OS right, trying to find the right spot to dig holes. We hear him digging and moving briskly between the two. He's puffed out but he has a mission. He circles the swimming area – the distance between two holes. He measures the distance in the area between by pacing. He 'swims' the surface between the two. He gets to his feet, howls at the cold, and stands still.*

Scene Two

The front office.

Two desks, one belonging to DR ERICH *and one to* LISA, *and three chairs. On* LISA'S *desk a small telephone switchboard and a pile of* DR KATSCHER'S *recently discarded clothes. A picnic basket sits beside* ERICH'S *desk.*

OSKAR *stands, still and cold in his coat, in the centre of the office.* LISA *sits behind her desk.* ERICH *stands by his.*

OSKAR   I'm so cold.

ERICH   Whose fault is that?

LISA   Oskar.

           (ERICH *moves plants from the edge of the
           conservatory entrance away towards the
           heater.* LISA *moves to* OSKAR, *taking his coat
           off.*)

ERICH   (*to* OSKAR) Do you want the plants to die?
           Well do you?

LISA	Don't shout at him.
ERICH	Why did you leave the conservatory door open? If you must wander about on the ice keep the bloody cold out there with you. Over here, Lisa – where it's warm.
LISA	Do you have to swear? (*To* OSKAR.) Come . . . here . . .

(LISA *pushes* OSKAR *towards the warmth.*)

ERICH	In the circumstances. Yes. No – not him. The plants. Bring me the plants.

(ERICH *nudges* OSKAR *away.* LISA *fetches the plants.*)

ERICH	Frost kills seedlings. You know that – I've told you – told you a hundred times – haven't I?

(LISA *takes* OSKAR'S *coat off and drapes it over* ERICH'S *desk.*)

LISA	Take your coat off. You're freezing – here.

(LISA *warms* OSKAR *with a brisk rub. The switchboard buzzes and lights up,* LISA *moves towards it.*)

ERICH	Lisa bring the others – the plants.

(LISA *moves towards the conservatory.*)

ERICH	And answer the phone – and bring me that cloth. Quickly.

(LISA, *unsure of which command to follow, stands still, flummoxed.* OSKAR, *noticing this, picks up a cloth from* ERICH'S *desk and hands it to him.* LISA *picks up the headset, places one earpiece to her ear and picks up the receiver.*)

ERICH   Let's hope we can save them.

             (ERICH *hands a pot to* OSKAR.)

LISA   Hello, State Hospital for hereditaries and
             incurables . . . Fraulein Mootz speaking . . .

ERICH   Look at this one. Already with fungal disease.
             Poor thing.

LISA   One moment – I'll see if he's available. Dr
             Erich . . .

ERICH   Very common in larkspur. You have to keep an
             eye out.

LISA   Its Frau Fischer . . . She wants to talk about her
             boy – Hans?

ERICH   No.

LISA   I'm sorry Frau Fischer . . . (*Switching phone
             lines.*) Please hold, caller . . . (*Switching back
             to Frau Fischer.*) He's not available . . .

             (ERICH *drops a pot.*)

ERICH   Damn it – pick it up for me. I said pick it up.

             (OSKAR *picks the pot up.* ERICH *steadies his
             shaking hand.*)

LISA   No he's not available . . . Yes . . . Goodbye . . .
             (*Hanging up – to* ERICH.) For pity's sake.

ERICH   Sclerotium rot yellows the leaves and wilts the
             plant. See?

LISA   (*picking up the second caller*) Good afternoon
             State Hospital . . . One moment please . . . Dr
             Erich . . .

ERICH   These two need urgent surgery.

(OSKAR *moves two plant pots to* ERICH'S *desk.*)

LISA   Herr Kluge enquires after his niece, Gretchen.

(ERICH *shakes his head.*)

LISA   I'm sorry Herr Kluge . . . Dr Erich is indisposed, I can't –

ERICH   In consultation.

LISA   Yes . . . In consultation . . . And your number is? (*Writing.*) Yes . . . Of course. (*Hanging up.*)

(LISA *clears spilled earth from the floor.*)

LISA   You haven't answered the phone for a fortnight.

ERICH   I'm not speaking to patients' families.

LISA   You want me to do it? Again.

ERICH   There's a list. Here. (*Handing list to* LISA.) Look it's . . . When you have time. When you . . . Please . . .

(*The switchboard buzzes again and a red light flashes.* LISA *looks to* ERICH *then flicks a switch.*)

LISA   Hello?

ERICH   There is always a choice, Oskar. The easiest course would be to simply dispose of the sick plants and allow the stronger ones to flourish. But I am a Doctor. Not a god. So I will try to save the sickly plant. Yes?

OSKAR   Yes.

LISA   You won't succeed. (*Pushing* ERICH *out of her way as she puts a pot into the entrance way to the conservatory.*)

ERICH   You tell me – What is the best choice – to let them live . . . Or to let them die?

OSKAR   To . . . die.

ERICH   Why you . . .

(ERICH *chases* OSKAR *around the office, play fighting, they both laugh.*)

LISA   Stop it. Stop it. I said STOP IT.

(ERICH *and* OSKAR *stop suddenly.* OSKAR *moves to look towards the conservatory door.* ERICH *composes himself and sits behind his desk.* LISA *picks up a notepad.*)

LISA   Oskar will always make the last of two choices, you know that.

ERICH   Rubbish.

LISA   Oskar – is it cold outside or is it hot?

OSKAR   Hot.

ERICH   He's joking with you.

LISA   (*touching* ERICH'S *desk*) Is this a desk or a chair?

OSKAR   A chair

ERICH   Very good, very good Oskar.

LISA   Is Dr Erich a doctor or a drunken fool?

OSKAR   He's a drunken fool.

ERICH   Eh?

OSKAR   – An idiot.

ERICH   Steady . . .

              (OSKAR *gestures rudely to* ERICH *who moves
              towards him.*)

LISA   That's enough.

ERICH   He's playing with us Lisa – smarter than we
              know, eh Oskar? You need to lighten up. You
              give yourself away.

LISA   Oskar, hang this up please.

              (LISA *hands* OSKAR'S *coat to him, he looks
              towards the conservatory and puts his coat on.
              The sound of a splash, off stage.*)

OSKAR   Hey.

LISA   (*looking towards the lake*) Oskar, what is it?

ERICH   (*looking towards the lake*) It's Dr Katscher.
              He's on the ice.

Scene Three

On the ice.

A splash, off stage. OSKAR *watches the surface of the ice. A
dark shape moves beneath.* OSKAR *watches and counts as*
KATSCHER'S *shadow moves under the ice.* OSKAR *'counts' to
eight.*

Scene Four

The front office.

OSKAR *stands in the office,* DR ERICH *and* LISA *watching him.*

LISA   Eight?

OSKAR   Eight.

ERICH	Eight seconds is not so good. I remember when he could do it in six.
LISA	Swimming between holes in the ice. It's insane.
ERICH	All in the name of science.
LISA	You need to stay indoors – do you hear me Oskar? You stay here. It's dangerous out there.
ERICH	It's dangerous everywhere. Haven't you noticed?
	(LISA *shakes* OSKAR *roughly out of his coat.*)
LISA	(*hanging* OSKAR'S *coat on the back of her chair*) How much longer will Dr Katscher be here?
ERICH	Overnight. His business is tomorrow morning. As usual.
LISA	It's not usual. There's nothing usual about it.
ERICH	Don't start.
LISA	We only have a handful of patients left here.
ERICH	My head is pounding.
LISA	A handful including Oskar.
ERICH	You think I don't know that?
LISA	– We can't pretend . . .
ERICH	My nerves are shredded . . .
LISA	So what will you do?

(*Aware of the red light flashing on the switchboard,* LISA *flicks the switch and picks up the headset and receiver.*)

ERICH   Nothing. I will do nothing. And so will you.

(*A silence.*)

LISA   Good afternoon, State Hospital for hereditary and incurable diseases . . .

ERICH   Come here. Look.

(ERICH *pulls* OSKAR *towards the plants.*)

LISA   Clara, its six o'clock . . .

ERICH   Where is she? The ward hasn't been medicated.

LISA   One moment . . . Do you want to talk to her?

(ERICH *waves his hand at* LISA *intimating 'no'.*)

ERICH   Her wages will be docked.

LISA   What . . . speak up? I can't . . . Hello . . . Clara speak clearly, I can't . . . What's the . . .

(ERICH *grabs the headset from* LISA.)

ERICH   Clara, its Dr Erich . . . I know one forgets the time when one is whoring for Hitler but there are patients waiting to be fed . . . I said . . . Hello . . . hello – Clara?

OSKAR   Clara?

(ERICH *replaces the handset.*)

LISA   Something was wrong. She's normally so reliable.

ERICH   She's jumped onto the back of a Wermacht
             man's scooter and forgotten the time.

LISA   You should have let her speak.

ERICH   You can cover for her, Lisa.

LISA   Me?

ERICH   We'll get a replacement. Tomorrow. Or the
             day after.

LISA   I'm not qualified.

ERICH   Nursing is kindness and drugs.

LISA   I don't even have a first aid certificate.

ERICH   You can do it standing on your head. Don't
             make a fuss. Not tonight, please. Oskar can
             help you, can't you Oskar? Be as
             indispensable as he is − yes?

             (ERICH *drapes his stethoscope around* OSKAR'S
             neck.)

LISA   Don't be ridiculous. What are you doing?

ERICH   What's the harm?

LISA   You're playing with fire.

KATSCHER   (*off*) Erich . . . Erich . . .

             (LISA *takes the stethoscope off* OSKAR'S *neck.*
             KATSCHER *enters, invigorated, wet, robe
             open, delirious with endorphins.*)

KATSCHER   I AM A SUPERMAN!

             (KATSCHER *picks* LISA *up and spins her around.
             She screams.*)

KATSCHER   I AM A MOUNTAIN BEAR!

(KATSCHER *lunges at* OSKAR *and spins him around.* OSKAR *laughs.*)

KATSCHER I AM A COLLOSUS!

(KATSCHER *moves towards* ERICH *as if to spin him around.*)

ERICH Not colossus enough.

KATSCHER Seven seconds. I am the seven second champion.

ERICH Eight.

KATSCHER What?

OSKAR Eight seconds.

(KATSCHER *laughs and clutches* ERICH *around the shoulders.*)

KATSCHER My heart is bursting with life. Feel it . . . Here . . . Feel it . . .

(KATSCHER *grabs* ERICH'S *hand and places it against his chest.*)

KATSCHER (*offering his chest*) Fraulein Mootz?

LISA Yes. Yes. (*Declining.*)

(OSKAR *approaches* KATSCHER *and puts his hand on his heart.* KATSCHER *puts his hand over* OSKAR'S *then pushes him away.*)

KATSCHER You . . . (*To* OSKAR.) . . . Here . . . Feel . . .That's life. As it should be. Boom-boom . . . Boom-boom . . .

(KATSCHER *moves away from* OSKAR.)

KATSCHER   Do you know pretty Lisa, that Erich used to
                beat me?

LISA   That surprises me.

KATSCHER   He was always the first one in the water back at
                Heidelberg.

ERICH   Times change. You can have the heroics. I'll
                have the beer and sausages.

KATSCHER   He could swim like a fish. He could outrun me.
                Out climb me and after a night on the town with
                the village girls he could out –

ERICH   Lisa, will you see to the wards. Check all is in
                order. Attend to the epileptics. Here.

                (KATSCHER *hands charts to* LISA, *she drops
                them.* KATSCHER *helps her to pick them up.*)

KATSCHER   Where is nurse Clara?

ERICH   What?

LISA   She's . . . She's . . .

ERICH   Called in sick.

KATSCHER   So you are the angel tonight. Spread your
                wings of mercy little Fraulein Mootz. (*He
                kisses her hand.*) We'll raise a glass together
                later – yes?

                (LISA *exits.* OSKAR *watches* KATSCHER.)

KATSCHER   Hurry Erich. Before I become disgustingly
                warm.

                (KATSCHER *clears the top of* ERICH'S *table, sits
                on it and pulls open the top of his robe.* ERICH
                *finds his equipment bag adeptly, and finds a
                thermometer which he pushes towards*
                KATSCHER'S *mouth.*)

ERICH   Are these experiments strictly necessary?

KATSCHER   Rectal Erich, an oral thermometer won't do.

                (KATSCHER *finds rectal thermometer in* ERICH'S
                bag and inserts it.)

KATSCHER   Haven't you heard?

                (ERICH *opens up his blood pressure box,
                moving the cuff up* KATSCHER'S *sleeve and
                inflating.*)

ERICH   You're forty years old, for God's sake.

KATSCHER   We need to know how long our airmen can
                tread the icy water in the northern territories.

ERICH   Sit still.

KATSCHER   Before their daring little dicks fall off. Ouch –
                careful. It's too tight.

ERICH   You may think you're still an athlete but your
                lungs will know their age.

KATSCHER   Speak for yourself.

                (ERICH *applies his stethoscope to the pressure
                band.*)

ERICH   I thought you were racial hygiene. You said
                military research was for the fanatics.

KATSCHER   Hypothermia is intrinsically interesting.

ERICH   Is it.

KATSCHER   Himmler wants servicemen who can withstand
                the cold. And what Himmler wants Himmler
                gets.

ERICH   I thought he wanted everyone to be six-foot-
             four with blue eyes.

KATSCHER   Lose the belly and you're a poster boy.

ERICH   Chest.

             (ERICH *places stethoscope on* KATSCHER'S *chest
             and listens.*)

KATSCHER   Can you believe those nutrition and agriculture
             dummies have been dunking monkeys in iced
             water for the past six months?

ERICH   Hypothermia research is uniquely dependent
             on human test subjects. Rats, pigs and apes
             react to cold differently. We knew that years
             ago.

KATSCHER   Exactly. Dr Sigmund Rascher is beginning
             some ground-breaking work . . .

ERICH   (*looking at his watch*) You can check it now.

             (KATSCHER *takes the thermometer out.*)

KATSCHER   Truly. Exciting work. Brave work. This time
             not monkeys but men. And I intend to be a part
             of it.

ERICH   Men?

KATSCHER   All the test subjects we want with no need for
             restraint. Imagine it. Experimentation with no
             limits.

ERICH   Vasodilatation has increased blood flow to
             roughly three thousand millilitres per minute.
             Judging by the feel of you there is . . .

             (KATSCHER *looks at the thermometer.*)

KATSCHER   Minimal vasoconstriction. Core temperature
                  thirty-five degrees. I can't get bloody cold
                  enough. I need the chill of death.

                  (KATSCHER *leaps up and pulls his robe back
                  on. He searches in* ERICH'S *drawer*.)

ERICH   It'll come soon enough.

KATSCHER   War presents opportunity. We need to push
                  the boundaries to find the answers. There's
                  never been a better time for medical research –
                  more and more freedom, that's what we have –
                  you could make your name, Erich.

ERICH   Get your hands out of there.

KATSCHER   Begrudge your old friend a cigar?

                  (KATSCHER *pulls a cigar out of a box in the
                  drawer.* LISA *enters*.)

LISA   Dr Erich, the patients are fractious.

KATSCHER   Dear. Oh dear.

LISA   Margarete has spilled water on her blanket and
                  the paddles haven't been charged in the
                  treatment room.

ERICH   Food. They need some food. That's what they
                  need.

KATSCHER   Nonsense.

ERICH   (*to* KATSCHER) We don't receive enough.

KATSCHER   They need pacification. The warm deep kiss of
                  drug-induced sleep.

                  (ERICH *gathers up his equipment*.)

LISA   Please hurry.

(LISA *exits*.)

KATSCHER   Is that Luminal?

ERICH   No, Scopolamine. Five milligrams should do it.
Oskar, come.

KATSCHER   Be generous and give them ten. Leave him here
with me. It's fine. Go. Go. Minister great
healer.

ERICH   It won't take long.

(ERICH *exits*.)

KATSCHER   Where does he keep his drink? I need a drink.
Find it for me.

(OSKAR *finds bottle in* ERICH'S *desk. He hands
it to* KATSCHER.)

KATSCHER   You're strong. A broad back. Some muscle.
The seven second champion salutes you.
Come, you can help me to dress. You will be
my butler, yes? My trousers. Give me my
trousers.

(KATSCHER *pulls off his robe.* OSKAR *picks up*
KATSCHER'S *trousers from the desk and moves
towards him.*)

KATSCHER   (*holding up bottle*) No hands. I have no
hands. I need assistance. Help me.

(OSKAR *holds out the trousers for* KATSCHER *to
step into and tries to do them up.* KATSCHER
bats him off.)

KATSCHER   That's enough. My shirt. And my tie.

(OSKAR *helps* KATSCHER *into his shirt and
drapes his tie around his neck and returns to
the pile of clothes.*)

KATSCHER   What a good servant you are. Jacket.

               (OSKAR *passes* KATSCHER *his jacket.* KATSCHER
               is dressed in full SS uniform.)

KATSCHER   Now my cap. I said give me my cap.

               (OSKAR *picks up* KATSCHER'S *cap from the desk
               and puts it on. He salutes.*)

OSKAR   Heil Hitler.

               (KATSCHER *takes the cap from* OSKAR.)

KATSCHER   What should I do? Laugh or cry?

OSKAR   Cry.

KATSCHER   I don't think so.

               (KATSCHER *turns his back on* OSKAR *as* OSKAR
               picks up KATSCHER'S *gun from its holster on
               the desk. He points it at* KATSCHER. KATSCHER
               turns.)

KATSCHER   Give that to me.

               (KATSCHER *approaches* OSKAR. OSKAR *backs
               away still pointing the gun at* KATSCHER.)

KATSCHER   You're going to shoot me? In Erich's office?
               Think of the consequences. The mess. You
               shoot me here. The bullet passes through. At
               the front a tiny hole but at the back. Blood all
               over the place. It would take a week to scrub
               me away. And then the body. What will you do
               with the body? You have to consider disposal.
               Killing isn't a moment it's a process. It must be
               clean . . . Enough . . . Come on . . .

               (KATSCHER *approaches* OSKAR, OSKAR *backs
               away.*)

OSKAR   (*shouting*) Bang . . . Bang . . .

(KATSCHER *clutches his chest. He laughs.*
OSKAR *puts the gun on* ERICH'S *desk.* KATSCHER
picks it up.)

KATSCHER   You may be very entertaining to have in the
            office but you really are life unworthy of life,
            aren't you?

ERICH   (*off*) I SAID NO VISITORS . . .

LISA   She didn't make an appointment.

            (ERICH *and* LISA *enter.*)

ERICH   I don't want to see anyone . . .

LISA   She just arrived.

KATSCHER   Is there a problem?

ERICH   Apologies Helmut, I said no appointments but
            there seems to . . .

ERICH   Be a difficulty with communicating . . .
        }
LISA   It's not my fault. I can't stop.

            (KATSCHER *picks up the basket by* ERICH'S
            desk.)

KATSCHER   I've brought Cognac. French chocolate. Cold
            meats and cigarettes. We can celebrate. Have
            an enjoyable evening before our business
            tomorrow. All work and no play makes Erich a
            very neurotic Doctor.

ERICH   I'm sorry Helmut, I said no visitors but . . .

KATSCHER   You tend to your meeting. It's fine. I'll go for a
            walk by the lake and look back at your Valhalla
            in the icy fog. (*Handing bottle to* ERICH.) Here.
            Drink deep. You evidently need it.

(KATSCHER *exits*.)

ERICH   I can't see anyone. Not relatives. Not now.

LISA   You can. And you must. Oskar, here.

             (LISA *arranges chairs.* ERICH *finds glass and
             pours schnapps – he drinks quickly.*)

LISA   Ready?

ERICH   Wait. Give me some time.

             (ERICH *pours another glass and downs it.*)

LISA   Drinking won't help.

ERICH   How can I do this work without drink? Some
             time please. Just to . . .

LISA   Alright.

             (LISA *exits.* ERICH *drinks from the bottle,
             gasping between gulps.* OSKAR *pulls the bottle
             away from him.* ERICH *pulls keys from his
             pocket and opens a drawer in his desk. His
             movements are frenetic and jerky.* ERICH *takes
             out three cardboard boxes from his drawer
             and checks them for identification.* ERICH *finds
             the box he is looking for and puts the other
             boxes back into the drawer. He finds a handful
             of buff envelopes in the drawer sorting
             through them, looking at names, and thinking
             he has found the one he needs places it next to
             the box. He revises his choice, checks the
             writing on the front and places his final
             choice next to the box. He locks his drawer.
             He takes the bottle from* OSKAR, *drinks and
             hides the bottle behind his desk. He places
             the box on* LISA'S *desk then changes his mind
             and places it in the centre of his desk. He spits
             into his hand and slicks his hair down He
             stands and tucks the box under his arm, the
             envelope in his hand. He faces the entrance*

*way, ready to receive his visitor. He breathes
deeply. He suddenly passes the box and
envelope to* OSKAR *and picks up the bottle
again from its hiding place behind the desk.
He lifts the bottle to his lips.* LISA *enters.*)

LISA   Frau Poppendick.

(ERICH *chokes on his drink and moves towards*
OSKAR *with the intention of taking the box and
envelope from him –* FRAU POPPENDICK *enters
and* ERICH *freezes. She is a formidable
presence with a huge energy, carrying a large
tart on a plate.*)

FR POPPENDICK   Heil Hitler.

ERICH   (*mumbling*) Heil Hitler.

OSKAR   Heil Hitler.

ERICH   (*indicating chair*) Please Frau . . .

FR POPPENDICK   (*ignoring chair*) Is today not the most
                munificent one, Dr Erich?

ERICH   Munificent?

FR POPPENDICK   Have you heard the latest bulletin? On the
                wireless?

ERICH   The news? No I don't listen to . . .

FR POPPENDICK   Tronheim and Oslo have fallen.

ERICH   They have? Well that is . . .

FR POPPENDICK   And Bergen is on the brink . . .

ERICH   So quick. I . . .

FR POPPENDICK   Of total capitulation.

ERICH   Total . . .

FR POPPENDICK Capitulation.

ERICH Capitulation. Yes.

FR POPPENDICK Victory in Norway is within our grasp.

ERICH Please sit, Frau . . .

FR POPPENDICK An advance division has begun the process of securing the flow of iron ore from the mines at Kiruna.

ERICH Iron ore. Iron ore you say?

FR POPPENDICK Isn't that magnificent?

ERICH Magnificent. Yes.

FR POPPENDICK On every street our beautiful young men are greeted with kisses and salutations to the Führer. It can only be a matter of time before destiny is fulfilled and the strong fist of the Reich is felt also across the face of France and Belgium. All hail to the courageous troops. All hail to the swelling of the Reich. Heil Hitler.

OSKAR Heil Hitler.

FR POPPENDICK Heil Hitler.

OSKAR Heil . . .

(ERICH *stands and ushers* FRAU POPPENDICK *into a chair.*)

ERICH Please sit, Frau Poppendick. Please. Please.

(FRAU POPPENDICK *hands the tart to* ERICH.)

FR POPPENDICK Apple and blackberry tart with a marzipan gonad. The pastry is short. The berries sour.

(ERICH *dithers with the plate,* LISA *takes it from him and places it on her desk.* ERICH *sits.*)

ERICH   From the Reich's mothers service?

FR POPPENDICK   No the BDM, Doctor Erich. My young girls.
                 On Tuesdays it is the BDM.

ERICH   Of course. Forgive me. And how are the
                 virtuous daughters of the Reich?

FR POPPENDICK   The Faith and Beauty Society.

ERICH   Faith and beauty. Yes.

FR POPPENDICK   Last night we made cakes and discussed the
                 reproductive organs.

ERICH   Indeed. With success?

FR POPPENDICK   I am making some progress with the baking.

ERICH   I see.

FR POPPENDICK   Doctor, you and I recognise the need for girls
                 to embrace motherhood for the sake of the
                 Fatherland. Our repatriated countries must be
                 peopled with Aryans as rapidly as possible.

ERICH   I've read the articles. Yes. The directives are
                 febrile. The need is patently pressing. Frau
                 Poppendick, I . . .

FR POPPENDICK   It's an obligation. These girls are the bloom of
                 Germany. Blonde, blue eyed, strong and
                 healthy. The key to continued perfection lies
                 between their thighs.

ERICH   Between their . . .

FR POPPENDICK   The beautiful must procreate. We know this.
                 Short sightedness, deafness, corpulence,
                 dipsomania and all graver manner of illness and
                 ugliness will become things of the past. Bred

out of the gene pool. What a paradise we are
making. It's a paradise, isn't it? A paradise?

(*A silence.* FRAU POPPENDICK *evidently wants
an answer. In desperation* ERICH *laughs.*
OSKAR *laughs too.*)

FR POPPENDICK   I told them to make as many children as
possible. Because that is the right thing to do.
Isn't it? To find exquisite square-jawed men
and produce at least four offspring in order to
ensure the continued quality of the national
stock. The genetically fit must not remain
childless. Isn't that right Fraulein Mootz?

LISA   Yes. Of course.

FR POPPENDICK   We must all play our part, standing up or lying
down we have our duty to do. Yes. A duty.

ERICH   You are indeed a most dutiful woman, Frau
Poppendick. How many children do you have?

LISA   Dr Erich.

FR POPPENDICK   Eight.

(FRAU POPPENDICK *has a sudden catastrophic
realisation.*)

FR POPPENDICK   Seven.

(FRAU POPPENDICK *holds her hands to her head
and makes a strange uncontrolled sound.*
ERICH *is paralysed and looks to* LISA *for help.*)

LISA   Frau Poppendick, I am very sorry for your loss.
I was fond of Franz and shocked to hear of his
death. He was in good health and happy when
he left here last month.

ERICH   Lisa.

FR POPPENDICK   Yes. He was.

ERICH   The Hadamar Institute has an excellent
                         reputation.

FR POPPENDICK Yes.

ERICH   Your son was – selected – for transfer because
                         it was considered with his difficulties that he
                         would benefit from the therapies on offer.
                         Water treatment. Herbal remedies. Comfortable
                         beds and exquisite medication. I hope you
                         accept that we did everything we could for him
                         while he was in our care and that we are
                         confident similar high standards were
                         maintained at the Hadamar . . .

FR POPPENDICK (*raising her hand*) Stop.

LISA   Frau Poppendick?

FR POPPENDICK Should I ever become incurably ill. I don't make
                         a distinction between mental and physical
                         illness. I would consider it a blessing if a kind
                         doctor . . . Gave me a dose . . . releasing me
                         from everything. Wouldn't you?

                         (*A question beyond the question has been
                         asked.* ERICH *looks to* LISA *for help. A silence.*)

ERICH   Don't trouble yourself with such thoughts,
                         Frau Poppendick, at a time like this.

FR POPPENDICK I have watched the care which you gave to my
                         Franz over the years but we all know where we
                         stand now, don't we? When life is a burden to
                         others. When life has no quality or use. When
                         days are filled with useless eating while
                         soldiers starve at the front. Surely it would be
                         quite natural . . . these days . . . to give an
                         injection? To take away the pain?

ERICH   Doctors save life. They don't take it.

LISA   Frau Poppendick, we . . .

ERICH   Oskar.

                         (ERICH *beckons* OSKAR *to give the box and
                         letter to* FRAU POPPENDICK.)

ERICH   The institute cremates immediately to inhibit
                         the spread of infection. His ashes. And his
                         certificate of death. My condolences.

                         (OSKAR *hands the box and the envelope to*
                         FRAU POPPENDICK. *She touches his face and
                         kisses his forehead.*)

FR POPPENDICK Such a small box. He was nearly two metres
                         tall. Such a small box.

ERICH   Good afternoon.

                         (ERICH *sits behind his desk and tends to a
                         plant.*)

FR POPPENDICK What was the cause of death?

ERICH   Franz was severely disabled, Frau Poppendick.

FR POPPENDICK He was yes but what killed him?

ERICH   What? I . . . It's contained within the certificate
                         . . . It's . . . It's in there. In the . . . Have a
                         pleasant afternoon. Goodbye.

FR POPPENDICK I joined the party in 1933. How far we have
                         come. How much we have achieved. We are
                         creating a better world. A cleaner one. A purer
                         one. (*Whispering to* ERICH.) What sacrifices we
                         have to make, Doctor. Heil Hitler.

OSKAR   Heil Hitler.

FR POPPENDICK Enjoy the cake.

                         (FRAU POPPENDICK *exits.*)

OSKAR   Heil Hitler.

             (ERICH *advances on* OSKAR, *he pushes him.*)

ERICH   Stop doing that – Its not funny – You'll laugh
             yourself into the grave, do you hear me? Do
             you hear me?

             (ERICH *shakes* OSKAR *roughly, they fight.*)

OSKAR   Get off me.

LISA   Leave him alone. Control yourself. Get a grip.
             Listen to me. Get a grip.

             (ERICH *backs away.*)

             Go and keep your guest company. Go. Get out.
             Get out I said. I said get out.

             (ERICH *grabs his bottle and exits towards the
             lake.*)

             Oskar. Oskar – come on. We are having a
             party. A party. Yes? Lay out the cloth. The
             food. The drink. Come on it's a party. Make
             everything nice. Like Christmas. Like a
             birthday. Yes.

             (OSKAR *sets to work with the picnic basket,
             takes items off the top of* ERICH'S *desk, lays out
             the cloth and lays food items out.* LISA *picks
             up the 'list' from* ERICH'S *desk and crosses to
             her switchboard. She puts on her headset and
             dials a number.* OSKAR *begins to dance.*)

LISA   Hello Herr Kluge? . . . It's Fraulein Mootz . . .
             Yes . . . Herr Kluge, I regret to inform you that
             Gretchen has passed away at the Hadamar
             institute . . . Yes . . . Her ashes and certificate
             of death are here for you to pick up at your
             convenience . . . Good evening.

(LISA *hangs up rapidly. She dials another number.*)

LISA   Hello is that Frau Fischer? Frau it's . . . Yes . . . No . . . Frau Fischer, please let me . . . Hans has passed away, I'm sorry . . . At the Hadamar, yes . . . His ashes and certificate of death are . . . Please . . . Good afternoon.

(LISA *slams the receiver down.* OSKAR *notices this.* LISA *begins to dial another number.* OSKAR *approaches her, stops her dialling and pulls her up to dance with him, he turns up the volume on the radio.* KATSCHER *enters and watches* OSKAR *and* LISA *dancing. He pulls* OSKAR *away and dances with* LISA. KATSCHER *runs his hands up* LISA'S *legs and under her skirt. She pulls away and turns off the radio.*)

OSKAR   Leave her alone.

(OSKAR *launches at* KATSCHER.)

KATSCHER   Quite the little Siegfried, aren't we? What powers do you have? Will you cast a ring of fire around her? How old are you now, little Lisa?

LISA   Twenty-nine.

KATSCHER   And no children? You are lax in your duty. Hitler says that motherhood is the woman's war. With every child she brings into the world she fights her own battle for the nation.

LISA   I'm not married.

KATSCHER   Marriage is an instrument of Christianity and Christianity is a branch of Judaism. Your leader cares not for the ring on your finger merely for the fruit of your womb. A childless woman is a corpse. In all the years I've been coming here I've never known you mention a

boyfriend. What's wrong with you, Fraulein
Mootz? What are you hiding?

LISA   Nothing. Nothing.

(ERICH *enters, drunk.*)

ERICH   Have you started without me?

KATSCHER   I believe you started without me – I saw you
reeling about in the summer house. (*To* OSKAR.)
You – serve the drinks. Cognac and beer.
Quickly.

(LISA *helps* OSKAR *prepare drinks.*)

KATSCHER   What a lucky man you are. Your own hospital.
To do with as you will. King of the Castle. I
tell you if you'd been stuck in general practise
for years like me you'd be counting your
blessings. Still everything is changed now
isn't it? Things will be different. I will have a
castle to rival yours.

ERICH   Oskar.

KATSCHER   But what an opportunity you have out here. I
tell you if I were in your shoes I would be in
seventh heaven.

ERICH   Go up to the ward now.

KATSCHER   No – leave him here and give him a drink.
Cognac. Large one.

ERICH   Beer, Lisa.

LISA   Oskar would you like cognac or beer?

OSKAR   Beer.

KATSCHER   You too, Fraulein Mootz. You need to loosen
up. Come . . . a toast.

        (KATSCHER *stands with his glass raised.* ERICH
        LISA *and* OSKAR *join him.*)

KATSCHER   To preventative health.

LISA   Preventative health

ERICH   Preventative health

        (OSKAR *drinks his beer down in one, all watch
        him.*)

KATSCHER   Give him more.

ERICH   No that's enough.

KATSCHER   Come on Erich, it's a party – more beer – more
        beer for . . . him. And another cognac for
        Erich.

        (LISA *and* OSKAR *attend to the drinks.*)

KATSCHER   This hospital is what, eighty – a hundred years
        old?

ERICH   A hundred and twenty. It was founded by a
        catholic charity for the safe incarceration of
        those considered incapable of normal life.

KATSCHER   I see. Designed and built with honest German
        sweat and muscle. What a lot of labour it must
        have taken. And cost. Let's not forget the
        cost.

ERICH   It was built on this hill by the lake to provide
        an airy and healthy environment. At its peak in
        the Weimar years there were eight hundred
        patients here.

LISA   Now it's virtually empty.

KATSCHER   I'm sorry Fraulein Mootz – what was that?

LISA   Nothing.

KATSCHER	All hereditaries. Idiots and the like? No lunatics?
ERICH	Some.
KATSCHER	Ah. Yes.
ERICH	And some idiots became lunatics.
KATSCHER	Naturally.
ERICH	Give me another, Oskar.

(OSKAR *brings* ERICH *another drink.*)

KATSCHER	None of the patients could be cured.
ERICH	Of course not.
KATSCHER	None would ever work. None would bear children. Dear oh dear.

(KATSCHER *reaches into his inside pocket, suddenly animated, he finds a photograph.*)

KATSCHER	Here. My boy. My Otto.
ERICH	He's grown. Practically a man.

(KATSCHER *shows the photograph to* LISA.)

KATSCHER	He attends the Reich school at Feldafing. He has recently achieved top marks for leadership, strength of character, toughness and decency. Look . . .

(KATSCHER *shows the photograph to* OSKAR.)

KATSCHER	Tall, long-skulled, a narrow face, a pronounced chin and a narrow nose with a high bridge. You see? Hair the colour of corn and widely spaced pale-coloured eyes. Isn't he beautiful? Isn't he perfect?

(OSKAR *pushes the photograph back towards*
KATSCHER.)

ERICH   You must be very proud of him.

KATSCHER   We should all be proud. Proud of our young
               people. They are the future. They deserve the
               best, don't they? Isn't that what we are doing?
               Shaping a better world for our young?

               (*A silence.*)

KATSCHER   But Erich, it troubles me. Deeply. How can our
               fine young boys and girls receive the best
               when it costs the state fifty thousand
               Reichsmarks for each genetically ill individual
               by the time they reach the age of sixty? Um?
               How do I explain that to my boy. My beautiful
               boy. Why should he struggle to be the best
               when the feeble are rewarded for their
               incapacity? This stuff gives me headaches.
               Bring me that pie.

               (OSKAR *brings* FRAU POPPENDICK'S *tart to*
               KATSCHER. *He breaks off a chunk and eats
               messily.* OSKAR *pours cognac for* ERICH.)

KATSCHER   These are difficult issues Erich, no one would
               question that – but we have the strength to
               address them, yes?

ERICH   Strength. Yes.

KATSCHER   The strength to be kind. To help nature along.
               To ensure the survival of the fittest, eh? Do
               you remember grade school, Erich? When we
               sat at the front together?

ERICH   It was a long time . . .

KATSCHER   (*to* LISA) There was this kid, Klaus, he had
               callipers on his legs. Really skinny. Couldn't

hear properly. Polio – you're familiar with the condition?

LISA   Yes. I'm familiar.

KATSCHER   You remember Klaus?

ERICH   Helmut, this is . . .

KATSCHER   Our dear teacher had some sort of mission and decided that Klaus should receive special treatment. You remember?

ERICH   We brought food for him.

KATSCHER   Yes we did. God knows how. None of us had anything. We begged our mothers . . . 'Please, it's for Klaus' . . . 'Please we must feed Klaus' . . . And every day Klaus would feast. Meat. Cake. Cheese. Until eventually he was fat. Really fat. And then one day Erich brought him an apple. Didn't you Erich?

ERICH   I should check on the ward.

            (ERICH *makes to leave*.)

KATSCHER   Sit down. I said sit down.

            (ERICH *sits*.)

KATSCHER   A big juicy green apple. And we sat in the playground – we were starving – and we watched Klaus eat. But he started to choke. Couldn't breathe. His eyes filled with panic. And we watched. And he struggled. And he died. But we didn't do anything, did we Erich?

ERICH   We didn't know what to do.

KATSCHER   We didn't call for help. We didn't clap him on the back. We chose not to do anything Erich, and you know it because deep in our hearts we

knew . . . We knew that what was happening
was right. Yes?

(*A silence.* ERICH *fills his glass. He fills* LISA'S
*glass too, although she intimates she doesn't
want him to, and fills* OSKAR'S *glass.*)

KATSCHER   Preventative health

LISA   Preventative health.

ERICH   Preventative health.

KATSCHER   Where's the dancing. Lisa dance for us.
Dance like you danced before.

(KATSCHER *grabs* LISA.)

LISA   No, I don't want to.

KATSCHER   You're refusing? What's the matter with you?

ERICH   Dance, Lisa. Dance.

(LISA *begins to dance.* OSKAR *dances too.*)

KATSCHER   Yes. Now imagine he is your lover. Show me
how you'd move. Show me. Christ, put some
feeling into it. Let's see a little more of you . . .

(KATSCHER *rips open* LISA'S *blouse, she covers
herself.*)

KATSCHER   I said dance. I want to be entertained. For
God's sake has everyone lost their sense of
humour? Life is for living, isn't it? For living.

(OSKAR *pushes* LISA *away and sings a loud
introductory and extended note –* KATSCHER *is
shocked into silence.*)

OSKAR   (*singing*) I love you
I need you
I touch you

I kiss you
I want you
I free you
I see you

(*to* KATSCHER) Let's swim under the ice
Let's breathe in twice
Then dive deep into the dark
One . . .Two . . . Three . . . Four . . . Five . . . Six
. . . Seven . . . EIGHT

I love you
I need you
I touch you
I kiss you
I want you
I free you
I see you (*To* KATSCHER.)
I kill you

OSKAR   (*pointing an imaginary gun at* KATSCHER) Bang
Bang!

(*A bell rings in the hallway OS.*)

KATSCHER   Is he goading me? Are you goading me?

ERICH   Who's at the front door at this time of night?

LISA   I'll go.

(LISA *exits.*)

ERICH   Come Helmut. Blood sausage. Chocolate.
More cognac – would you like to smoke a
cigar?

KATSCHER   You allow him to do this? To openly display
insubordination to his betters? You allow
underlife the freedom to poke fun?

ERICH   It will never happen again. Oskar, back to the
ward.

KATSCHER	No. No. Leave him here. He reminds me of everything we're fighting for. Tell him to sit down and shut up.
ERICH	He's joking . . . He's . . . Sit down, Oskar.
KATSCHER	And?
ERICH	And shut up.
KATSCHER	Christ, Erich. Come. Preventative health.
ERICH	Cheers.
KATSCHER	You remember the parties we used to have? With accordion and dancing. The eating competitions – you once managed two pounds of butter, remember that? Out on the terrace at midnight. Smoking and telling stories. You once ran through the wards dressed as a Valkirie . . . Playing with the dogs. Cards. Brandy and filthy stories, eh? Where has all the fun gone? Eh? Why can't we laugh in the same way? Me and Elsa and you and your . . .
ERICH	I prefer not to talk about the past, Helmut.
KATSCHER	She was a model of womanhood. She would have borne you fine sons Erich, I'm sure of it.
ERICH	She's dead and that's the end of it.

(ERICH *whistles the opening bars of the dance music played earlier and pours another drink.*)

KATSCHER	She didn't just die. She made the noblest sacrifice. She knew she was ill. She knew there was no hope. So to save everyone's trouble she drank a bottle of bleach.

(ERICH *forces* OSKAR *to dance with him.* KATSCHER *throws files violently onto the floor.* ERICH *and* OSKAR *stop.*)

KATSCHER   God, what an example. If only the elderly and
             infirm could make the same choice and save us
             the bother.

ERICH   Who was at the door?

KATSCHER   I've always admired you, my old friend. You're
             cleverer than me.

ERICH   Have another drink . . .

KATSCHER   No. No. Listen. You progressed quicker. You
             found your feet while I was thrashing about.
             They gave you this hospital. Times are
             changing Erich, and I want you to come with
             me. To help me. You know me I'm all ideas and
             passion. The analysis. The journals I'm just
             not cut out for . . . You can help me. My old
             friend. Yes? I need you. Please.

ERICH   What? I can't . . . What are you talking about?
             You don't need me.

KATSCHER   How much longer can you carry on here? Your
             patients will all go Erich, you know that.

ERICH   Go?

KATSCHER   To the Hadamar Institute. In time it will just be
             you and . . . whoever . . .

ERICH   But new patients . . .

KATSCHER   The world is changed. For the better. For us.
             Come with me. Come and work with me. Equal
             rank. Partners. We'll have our own laboratory.
             I'll do the lab work and you can write the
             papers. You'll get a lovely house – it's all part
             of the package. Women – women on tap – when
             was the last time, eh? Parties and perks like
             you've never known. Forget the war, this will
             be like peacetime on a consultant's wage.
             We're valued. And we get to do everything –

everything we've ever dreamed of. Come on Erich.

ERICH   What is it you dream of?

KATSCHER   Extremis. A removal of restriction.

ERICH   I dream of sleep.

KATSCHER   Come with me Erich. We'll be a great team.

ERICH   Where?

KATSCHER   Dachau. The concentration camp. Dr Rascher is a great guy. You'll love him. Such a sense of humour. He likes Wagner too, you can go to the camp concerts together. The Hypothermia Project. It's huge. And brilliant. It's the one – the career-maker. Cheers.

ERICH   Dachau?

KATSCHER   It'll be like old times. You me and a tank of cold water.

                 (*A silence.*)

ERICH   When I get up in the morning the first thing I think of is drink. My throat's parched and no amount of water can help. I brush my teeth and I vomit. I look at myself in the mirror and my heart shrivels. My hands shake. I sweat. I make my morning rounds drunk. I drop things. My signature is so erratic the pharmacist now accepts a cross. My synapses are shot to bits. I can't remember from one moment to the next. I can't bear any form of human interaction. I'm capable of violent mood swings and crushing apathy. Food has no taste and women no excitement. I'm frequently short-changed in shops because they think I'm none the wiser. My soul is sick. I'm not fit to dig graves. Why in God's name would you want to employ me?

KATSCHER   Because we think the same. That's all that counts. You're one of us.

ERICH   I'm sorry . . . I . . .

KATSCHER   Away from here you'll be a new man. A short – dry – holiday. I know just the place – and you'll be . . .

ERICH   Can I be honest. As an old friend?

KATSCHER   Of course. Of course.

            (ERICH *moves to sit next to* OSKAR.)

ERICH   I have a new crop of Chamomile in the conservatory which has been frost-bitten but I am enabling it to survive.

KATSCHER   You can have a garden. Many doctors and camp staff have gardens. Rascher himself grows the most lush blooms. Prize blooms. The best.

ERICH   Oskar helps me. With the plants. Don't you Oskar?

OSKAR   Yes.

KATSCHER   So?

ERICH   I don't want to come to Dachau. I couldn't do the job. It's not me. We don't . . . think the same.

            (*A silence.*)

KATSCHER   I'm a party member.

ERICH   I know . . .

KATSCHER   A member of the SS.

ERICH   Yes.

KATSCHER   What you have just told me is suggestive of
            sedition. I can report you.

ERICH   For being a drunk or for being a gardener?

KATSCHER   I could order you to come.

ERICH   Oh for God's sake, you can't really believe in it
            all? Hm? Didn't you once treat patients with
            no prejudice in the hope that they'd live?
            What's the matter with you? You've always
            been a pretty hopeless doctor. Write your
            papers for you? Papers? You? The great
            medical researcher? You're good for lancing
            boils Helmut, and that's just about it. You can
            go to hell. I'm not coming with you.

KATSCHER   Shut up. (*To* OSKAR.) You. Stand up. You
            need a cure, Dr Erich.

ERICH   Leave him out of it.

KATSCHER   A cure for your liberal bullshit. Your
            mechanistic materialistic Jewish communist
            ideology. (*To* OSKAR.) You laughed at me. He
            laughed at me and you allowed it to happen.

ERICH   Helmut . . .

KATSCHER   Let's see if you can beat seven seconds . . .
            Out on the lake . . . Yes?

ERICH   He can't swim Helmut, for Christ's sake . . .

KATSCHER   We need a length of rope. Out. Now. Go.

            (KATSCHER *exits*.)

ERICH   No . . . No . . . Wait . . .

            (ERICH *makes towards the door. He stops. He
            tries to move forwards. He stops. He pours a*

drink. He does nothing. He moves forwards
again and then does nothing. LISA *enters.*)

LISA   They're killing the patients.

ERICH   What?

LISA   They killed Hans. They killed Gretchen.
            They're killing everyone. At the Hadamar
            Institute.

ERICH   Ah . . . I have to . . .

            (*A silence.* ERICH *is still torn between moving*
            outside and staying inside. He doesn't move.)

ERICH   Nurse Clara? She was here?

LISA   She says they are killing the patients. Nurses.
            Doctors. At the Hadamar Institute. Where we
            transfer . . . They are killing the patients.

ERICH   Clara is unwell.

LISA   They are killing the patients.

ERICH   She is unhinged.

LISA   They are killing the patients. She witnessed it.

ERICH   How can I get up in the morning? How can I
            wash my face? How can I shave and eat my
            breakfast and go about my day and consult and
            heal and garden and read the paper go to the
            movies and drink schnapps when you tell me
            these things? I can't know these kind of things
            and continue to live.

LISA   You've managed so far.

ERICH   WHAT THE HELL WAS SHE DOING THERE?

            (ERICH *pours another drink.*)

LISA   She wanted to know what happened to our patients when they were transferred. She got through the guard post because she was wearing her uniform. And she couldn't easily be seen because of the black smoke coming from the chimney. She met the nurses there. Rough girls with bad manners.

ERICH   Milk maids and abattoir workers. That's all they can get up there.

LISA   She passed locked wards and other wards where people were starving.

ERICH   Shortages, Lisa, for God's sake we barely have enough here.

LISA   Being starved. To death. Bones pressing through skin.

ERICH   Some medical conditions can cause extreme emaciation.

LISA   There are rooms. In the basement. Two nurses attend. Always two nurses in case one becomes emotional. An injection is given. An overdose.

ERICH   That's enough.

LISA   They are building airtight chambers now. For gas. For gassing. For economies of scale.

       (*A silence.*)

LISA   What will you do?

KATSCHER (*off*) ERICH – GET OUT HERE – ERICH . . .

LISA   Now that you know?

       (ERICH *is caught and doesn't know where to go.*)

ERICH   I . . .

KATSCHER   (*off*) ERICH!

ERICH   What can I do? I'm just one man. What can I –

                 (LISA *slaps* ERICH *hard around the face.*)

LISA   Do something. Do something.

KATSCHER   ERICH – BRING THE ROPE . . .

                 (ERICH *exits.*)

Scene Five

On the ice.

KATSCHER *stands in front of* OSKAR, *a lantern in his hand, another at his feet. It's pitch dark and bitterly cold.*

KATSCHER   HURRY UP ERICH, WE'RE WAITING FOR
                 YOU . . .

                 (KATSCHER *checks* OSKAR'S *heart with
                 stethoscope and then his pulse.* OSKAR
                 shivers.)

OSKAR   It's cold.

KATSCHER   You'll be warm soon enough. Breathe deeply.
                 Now take your clothes off. Take them off.

                 (ERICH *enters carrying a length of rope.*)

ERICH   Helmut, what are you doing? It's freezing.
                 Pitch dark. Let's go inside. Stop this. Now.
                 It's insane.

KATSCHER   You have rope?

ERICH   I have this . . . I'm not sure how strong it will
                 be. If you really want to be sure of saving him
                 we could do with some proper . . . proper . . .

KATSCHER   Saving him? (*Laughing.*) I want to retrieve the
                 body, Erich. Post-mortem. That's where the
                 real learning is. We wait for no movement at
                 the end of the rope and then haul up the
                 recently deceased. If we can get the results
                 down in black and white we'll have an
                 advantage . . .

                 (OSKAR *has shed his clothes.*)

KATSCHER   (*pointing imaginary gun at* OSKAR) Bang . . .
                 bang . . . beat seven seconds, monkey boy . . .

ERICH   Wait . . . I'll do it . . .

                 (ERICH *begins to take off his clothes.*)

KATSCHER   What?

ERICH   I'll beat you. Hands down. Proper challenge
                 yes? What's the fun in watching him die. I'll
                 meet your time or beat it – how about that?

KATSCHER   Are you mad?

ERICH   Put your clothes on, Oskar. Before you catch
                 your death.

                 (OSKAR *puts his clothes back on.* ERICH *takes
                 his off.* ERICH *pulls rope from* OSKAR *and puts
                 it around his waist.*)

KATSCHER   You're out of condition, Erich. You've drunk
                 your body weight in alcohol tonight. The first
                 plunge of your head under the surface will
                 make you involuntarily breathe in. Your body
                 will cool in icy water twenty-five times faster
                 than in cold air. Your core temperature will
                 plummet. Heart lungs and that overworked liver
                 will starve and constrict. Your swimming stroke

will slow and you'll any sense of direction. You'll become disorientated and lose consciousness. You'll disappear beneath two feet of ice. Blades will bite your chest as you breathe in water. The moment before you die will be peaceful. You're really going to do this – for him?

OSKAR   No.

KATSCHER   There are three lanterns at the edge of the farther hole. With luck you'll be able to see a blur of light in the darkness.

KATSCHER   Seven seconds.

(ERICH *exits.* OSKAR *enters.*)

KATSCHER   Seven seconds is the time to beat. Come.

(KATSCHER *exits with* ERICH. *A splash OS.* OSKAR *watches the ice as a shape moves under it. He counts to six.*)

Scene Six

The office.

ERICH *lies on the floor shivering.* LISA *and* OSKAR *watch him from a distance. He turns over and sits up.*

ERICH   I'm so cold.

(LISA *throws a bath robe at him.*)

LISA   Who's fault is that?

(KATSCHER *walks through the office with* ERICH'S *clothes. He throws them at* ERICH. *He picks up* ERICH'S *keys from his trouser pocket and waves them at him, he puts them in his pocket.*)

KATSCHER   Congratulations. You are the six second
                champion.   I am beaten . . . Until tomorrow.

                (KATSCHER *exits*.)

ERICH   Get me a bloody drink . . .

                BLACKOUT.

ACT TWO

Scene One

The office.

The following morning. 9.00 AM. Bright sunlight pours into the office.

FRAU POPPENDICK *sits, motionless, a large handbag on her lap.* OSKAR *sweeps the floor, moving closer and closer to* FRAU POPPENDICK, *who doesn't move.* OSKAR *sweeps close to* FRAU POPPENDICK'S *feet, she doesn't move.* OSKAR *sweeps over* FRAU POPPENDICK'S *feet, she doesn't move.* OSKAR *waves his hand in front of* FRAU POPPENDICK'S *face, she doesn't move.* OSKAR *touches her. She doesn't move.*

LISA *enters, she is dressed fastidiously, her hair neatly pinned up, with her best shoes on.*

LISA	Oskar. What are you doing? Stop it.
	(OSKAR *moves away from* FRAU POPPENDICK *and continues sweeping.* LISA *arranges chairs.*)
LISA	My apologies, Frau Poppendick. I can't find him. I'm sure he won't be long. We have a meeting. An important meeting – he will be here soon I'm sure. Oskar, where is Dr Erich?
OSKAR	Dr Erich?
LISA	Have you seen him?
OSKAR	Yes.
LISA	So is he on the lake? At the nurses station? On the wards?
OSKAR	On the wards.
LISA	(*handing papers to* OSKAR) Here. I'll go and –

(Lisa *exits, bumping into* Katscher *as he
enters.* Oskar *puts papers onto chairs.*
Katscher *is in full uniform, looking sharp and
crisp. He barely looks at* Frau Poppendick *as
he crosses to* Erich's *desk and uses* Erich's
*keys to open a drawer. He takes out a handful
of files which he evidently needs to read
pressingly.*)

(Frau Poppendick *salutes strangely at*
Katscher. Katscher *ignores her and walks
past her towards the conservatory exit.* Frau
Poppendick *throws herself at* Katscher's *feet,
grabbing him around the ankles. He manages
to shake her off and exits.*)

(Oskar *helps* Frau Poppendick *to her feet and
returns her to her chair.* Erich *enters, half of
yesterday's half-man, dishevelled, unshaven,
still drunk and distracted. He notices his
open desk drawer and slams it shut with
violence. He repeats the violence shutting it
twice.* Oskar *moves to him to make him stop.*)

(Oskar *makes* Erich *become aware of* Frau
Poppendick. *He crosses to the centre of the
room.*)

ERICH   Ah. Frau . . . Popp-pippidonk Poppen . . .
            (*Clearing his throat and fighting the need to
            vomit.*) Heil Hitler.

OSKAR   Heil Hitler.

ERICH   I said Heil Hitler.

OSKAR   Heil Hitler.

ERICH   Frau . . . Popp . . . en . . . dick?

            (*A silence.* Frau Poppendick *remains
            immobile.*)

ERICH   I hear . . . I hear on the . . . I hear that our
               indomitable navy now has unfettered control of
               the Norwegian seas.

               (FRAU POPPENDICK *doesn't respond.*)

ERICH   The Norwegian seas . . . Yes . . . Our U-boats
               need no longer risk the straits of Dover or the
               Scottish coast . . . Which would apparently be
               – disastrous. The English infantry are no match
               for the arctic chill and it has been demanded
               that the Norwegians surrender immediately . . .
               Surrender, Frau Poppendick . . . That is good
               news – isn't it? A good resounding surrender.
               Yes.

               (*Still* FRAU POPPENDICK *doesn't respond.*)

ERICH   You will be celebrating with the girls of the
               league no doubt . . . There will be busy boiling
               ovens and febrile talk of Scandinavian sexual
               intercourse . . . Yes?

               (ERICH *feels nauseous. He finds a vase
               containing dead flowers. He throws the
               flowers out and drinks the water, covering
               himself with liquid. He wipes the excess from
               his face.*)

FR POPPENDICK Thirsty work. Murder.

               (*A silence.* ERICH *freezes. He chooses to
               ignore the statement. He crosses to his desk
               and sits behind it, the 'doctor' once more. He
               puts his stethoscope on, slicks his hair and
               breathes deeply trying to focus.*)

ERICH   We are in an increasingly strong position. If
               Norway can fall so quickly the rest of Europe
               will surely soon be ours. Triumph. Foot-
               stamping, table-thumping triumph, Frau, is a
               whisker away. A hair's breath. A drum's beat.

                  (FRAU POPPENDICK *is suddenly animated, a switch has been flicked.*)

FR POPPENDICK   I don't wish to keep you. I know your machine must function in its relentless manner.

ERICH   What? Machine? I . . . In these circumstances . . . My door is always open to you. Condolences, I . . .

FR POPPENDICK   Is that why it's so cold in here?

ERICH   The temperature has dropped. The conservatory door was left open. Bracing, isn't it? Stirs the soul. Quickens the blood. Yes.

FR POPPENDICK   You see this . . .

                  (FRAU POPPENDICK *takes off the cross which hangs around her neck and holds it out towards* ERICH.)

ERICH   It's a cross. A mother's cross . . .

FR POPPENDICK   A silver cross, Dr Erich. A silver cross. I am no longer a golden woman. It's virtually worthless.

                  (FRAU POPPENDICK *throws the cross at* OSKAR'S *feet. He picks it up and puts it on.*)

ERICH   Oh. I'm sorry, I . . .

FR POPPENDICK   The system is so efficient. The bureaucracy very swift. A stickler from the local party came to my door last night. All greased hair and rule book. Sweaty hands and a clerk's smile. You no longer have eight children, Frau. That's what he said to me. You no longer have eight children.

ERICH   Well there is some truth in –

FR POPPENDICK You are entitled only to the silver cross.

ERICH Ah. I see. I . . .

FR POPPENDICK It may as well be tin for what it's worth.

ERICH Yes. Tin. Not so . . .

FR POPPENDICK I'll no longer be entitled to the privileges. The respect. The Hitler Youth will not salute me in the street and at the butchers I won't be able to jump the queue.

ERICH The meat isn't up to much anyway . . . These days . . . when you can . . . If you . . . sorry.

(*A silence.* FRAU POPPENDICK *lapses into stasis again.*)

ERICH You will have to make up the numbers again. Yes? Keep your husband busy when he returns from the front. Follow your own teaching section leader. Open wide for Hitler.

FR POPPENDICK Yes.

ERICH I hear that once you bear ten children the Führer himself will be Godfather to the child. Imagine that. Imagine the cakes.

FR POPPENDICK Imagine. Yes.

ERICH Now there's your purpose. There's your ambition.

FR POPPENDICK I don't think so.

ERICH There is still time. You can eradicate the past with new life . . . Yes . . . New life . . . You say yourself there is no larger purpose in a woman's life than to provide children for the nation.

FR POPPENDICK   So long as they are not blind or deaf or
                crippled or not quite right in the head.

                (*A silence.*)

ERICH   (*looking at his watch*) Is that the time? We
                have an important . . . So much to . . . Patients.
                Yes . . . I must press on Frau. Take plenty of
                rest. Walk in the park. See a movie. Focus on
                your BDM girls and fill up the vacuum you feel
                with work. Work liberates us all. Heil Hitler.

OSKAR   Heil Hitler.

                (ERICH *stands*. FRAU POPPENDICK *takes an
                envelope from her bag and opens it up to find
                a hair pin which she holds up*.)

FR POPPENDICK   What is this Dr Erich? In your opinion?

                (FRAU POPPENDICK *holds out the hair pin*.
                OSKAR *takes it and hands it to* ERICH.)

ERICH   What? It's a pin. A metal clasp. The kind a
                young girl would use in her hair.

FR POPPENDICK   I went straight from here yesterday with the
                box you gave me. I held it close on the bus. I
                went indoors and picked up the urn I had
                already set aside. Lid off on a sheet of
                newspaper. The space was waiting on the
                mantelpiece. I opened the box and poured the
                ashes into the urn. And that pin fell out. Fell
                out of my Franz's ashes. My big fifteen year
                old boy. A girl's hair pin? A girl's hair pin?

ERICH   A mistake. A mix up. I imagine. An accident.

FR POPPENDICK   Perhaps.

ERICH   A nurse maybe or a technician . . . while
                packaging the clip fell from the hair into the . . .

FR POPPENDICK   It's burned to a crisp.

ERICH	I am convinced the utmost care was taken at the Hadamar Institute. We are all professional.
FR POPPENDICK	Professional what?
ERICH	Consider yourself lucky. Franz received care. He had . . . he was . . . Yes . . .
ERICH	Lucky . . .
FR POPPENDICK	Lucky?
ERICH	What do you take us for Frau Poppendick?
FR POPPENDICK	Killers, Dr Erich. Killers.

(*A silence.*)

ERICH	I forgive you. You are grieving. You don't know yourself.
FR POPPENDICK	Don't I?
ERICH	You may also be menopausal.
FR POPPENDICK	What?
ERICH	This kind of thing happens in crematoria every day of the week.
FR POPPENDICK	It does?
ERICH	And depressed. Morbid. You are morbid, Frau. Possibly borderline hysterical. Without examining you its hard to know but there may also be a physical cause. I will prescribe something to numb all of this unnecessary pain.

(ERICH *finds his prescription pad.*)

FR POPPENDICK	Will it kill me?

(*A silence.*)

ERICH   A sedative. To stop you feeling what you are
                    feeling.   You are not in a sound state. Think
                    of your other children. Your healthy children.
                    Why would you inflict this on them? You are a
                    fine German woman. All is well. All is good.
                    Here.

                    (ERICH *passes the prescription to* FRAU
                    POPPENDICK.)

ERICH   One tablet three times a day. Nothing will
                    touch you. Your emotions will be frozen. Its
                    for the best. Yes?

                    (FRAU POPPENDICK *wails*. ERICH *moves to her.*
                    OSKAR *moves towards her* – ERICH *gestures to
                    him to stay away*.)

ERICH   There. There. All will be well. Bake up a storm
                    Frau Poppendick, and allow yourself extra
                    sugar.

FR POPPENDICK Do you remember Franz, Dr Erich?

ERICH   Yes. Yes of course I do. He would help me in
                    the conservatory sometimes. Water the plants.
                    Collect up the pots. Very helpful.

FR POPPENDICK Yes he was.

ERICH   A happy soul. Always smiling and laughing.

FR POPPENDICK Apart from when he was so sick. You
                    remember. With the appendicitis?

ERICH   Yes I do. That was a challenge. I had to
                    operate swiftly.

FR POPPENDICK You removed his appendix yourself. You're
                    sure of that?

ERICH   Of course I'm sure. I'm not a surgeon. It was
                 tough. But he survived. I did it.

                 (FRAU POPPENDICK *stands and finds envelope in
                 her bag, suddenly dry eyed.*)

FR POPPENDICK   Here. Read this.

                 (FRAU POPPENDICK *hands death certificate to*
                 ERICH, *he reads.*)

FR POPPENDICK   The death certificate from the Hadamar
                 Institute. Franz died apparently of a ruptured
                 appendix. Almost exactly a year after you
                 removed it.

                 (*A silence.*)

FR POPPENDICK   I asked for the truth. You lied. You knew all
                 along. You doctors, what are you doing?

ERICH   I didn't know. I swear. I didn't know.

FR POPPENDICK   You did. You did and did nothing. And you do
                 nothing. And now there's nothing that can be
                 done. Its too late. This is how the world is.
                 This is our paradise. People boil in oil while
                 blocks of ice stand watching.

                 (*A silence.*)

FR POPPENDICK   Good day.

ERICH   Good day Frau Poppendick. Your cross.

FR POPPENDICK   He can keep it. It will be incinerated with the
                 rest.

                 (FRAU POPPENDICK *exits.* ERICH *drinks and
                 sings angrily with* OSKAR.)

OSKAR   (*singing*) I love you
                 I need you
                 I touch you

> I kiss you
> I want you
> I free you
> I see you

(KATSCHER *enters carrying the files.* ERICH *and*
OSKAR *stop. He crosses to* ERICH'S *desk and*
puts the files on top of it. He pulls at another
drawer and tries keys.)

ERICH   What are you doing?

KATSCHER   Why won't this drawer open? None of your
                 keys work.

ERICH   You have the necessary documentation.
                 There's nothing else to give you. You have it
                 all.

KATSCHER   The hereditary health cards make for hideous
                 reading. The patients you have left are a sorry
                 bunch indeed. You're shaking. Have a drink.

ERICH   There's nothing in there. Staff records.
                 Details. Not relevant. Not relevant to today's
                 selection.

KATSCHER   I'll be the judge of that.

ERICH   What do you mean?

KATSCHER   Christ – do you read these files? When did you
                 last look at them? Properly? Do you know
                 what you're treating? The photographs?
                 Jesus, what's wrong with you? Who in their
                 right mind would want to work with such
                 creatures? Um? A sadist I can understand.
                 Plenty of scope for that kind of game with a
                 subject of low intelligence. A sexual pervert
                 yes, an asylum like this offers opportunity but
                 a normal man – a talented doctor, that's what
                 you were – who enjoys working with morons?
                 What is it? Guilt? Or does it make you feel
                 superior? Think you're better than me, Erich?

With your conservatory and your tame patients
. . . It makes no sense. Makes no sense at all . . .

(KATSCHER *tries to force the drawer open*.)

ERICH   Get away from that drawer. Those papers are
               confidential. You can't just . . . You can't . . .

KATSCHER   You can't . . . You can't . . . You can't . . . I
               can, don't you see? I can do anything I want.
               Who's going to stop me? You? Him? I don't
               think so. Some of us, Erich, have the guts and
               sinews to be active in this life. The rest of you
               stew and fester in your sickly sweet passivity.
               The idea that we are somehow elevated by our
               capacity to pity is tedious and naïve. The
               imbecile becomes sacred. Ancient
               superstitious nonsense. When a bird flies into
               your window and breaks its neck do you leave
               it to die slowly? No you hear the thud and you
               go outside and wring its neck . . . quickly. In
               nature does the runt of the litter receive the
               cream of the crop? No. It's cast out . . . The
               best rise to the top and those at the bottom are
               disposable.

ERICH   It's not pity. It's value.

KATSCHER   Open this drawer. There is no value in –

ERICH   I've saved frostbitten plants that have cross-
               fertilised and generated fields of colour.

KATSCHER   Those fields of colour would bloom anyway
               without the need for a gardener. Nature does
               it.

ERICH   Blonde beautiful bodies will all die of
               something.

KATSCHER   They'll look pretty and sing wonderful songs
               before they do.

ERICH   (*indicating* OSKAR) He can sing.

(OSKAR *sings – a single, pure note. A silence.*)

KATSCHER   Open this drawer . . . Open this drawer now . . .

ERICH   No.

                (KATSCHER *breaks the lock with ferocious
                violence and finds the files he's looking for.*)

KATSCHER   You're a fool. And your card is marked.

                (LISA *enters.*)

LISA   The patients have been fed and medicated and
                are ready for your rounds, Dr Erich.

KATSCHER   I have some reading to attend to Fraulein
                Mootz. (*Holding up* LISA'S *file so she can see
                her name written on it.*) We start when I
                return. Give the six-second champion some
                charcoal, he looks like he's going to throw up.

                (KATSCHER *exits.*)

LISA   The staff records? He has the . . .

                (LISA *launches herself at* ERICH.)

LISA ⎫   What's the matter with . . .

OSKAR ⎬   Hey hey hey . . .

ERICH ⎭   Stop it, Lisa. This won't help. Stop it.

ERICH   We need to think clearly. Carry on as normal –
                you understand? Our best hope is that usual
                process is followed.

LISA   He'll find us out. Oskar is already doomed.

ERICH   Not necessarily.

LISA   After last night? You think he'll turn a blind
                eye? Don't be ridiculous

ERICH	Oskar. Sit. Listen to me.
	(OSKAR *sits*.)
ERICH	We can pack you a bag. Bread from the kitchen. Warm clothes. Walk by the edge of the lake and through the forest. On the other side is the village. Find a house. Ask for shelter.
LISA	They'll turn him in.
ERICH	Or the railway station. Go to the railway station and find a compartment.
LISA	And go where? How can he survive anywhere but here?
ERICH	Or I can give you some pills.
LISA	No. Stop it.
ERICH	It's your choice, Oskar. You can run or you can stay.
OSKAR	Stay.
LISA	For pity's sake. Oskar, you can stay or you can run?
OSKAR	Run.
LISA	You see? Give me a bag and some food and I'll take my chances.
ERICH	No.
LISA	I want to go let me go.
ERICH	I SAID NO. I need you.
LISA	What about me?

(ERICH *grabs* LISA *by the shoulders.*)

ERICH   Listen to me. Listen. The boy Katscher spoke
             about. The boy who choked. The apple. You
             remember.

LISA   What does it matter?

ERICH   I wanted to help him. I was ready to. I
             couldn't because none of the others . . . It
             wasn't what everyone was doing- do you see?
             My instinct was right. But I couldn't be
             different. Then. I couldn't . . .

LISA   And look where that's taken us. Get off get off
             me you coward.

             (LISA *shakes* ERICH *off.*)

ERICH   We will carry on. As normal. Fraulein Mootz. I
             said as normal. Come. Set up the meeting.

             (*Movement not normal. Preparation for a
             meeting. Activity is off centre.* ERICH *moves
             chairs and puts his jacket on. He takes his
             jacket off and puts it on again.* LISA *drops her
             papers and applies make up.* LISA *drops her
             papers again and picks them up.* OSKAR *clears
             desks. He dances and clears desks again.
             Although there's nothing there.* OSKAR *places
             a typewriter on* LISA'S *desk.* ERICH *drinks. All
             sit in their positions ready for the meeting to
             commence. All change positions. All change
             again.* ERICH *is sick.* KATSCHER *enters. He
             drops the files at his feet.*)

KATSCHER   Begin . . . the record . . .

             (*Snapping fingers at* LISA. *She types speech on
             her typewriter.*)

KATSCHER   Thursday, February 11th, 1940. Andernach
             State Hospital for hereditary and incurable
             diseases. In attendance Hauptsturmfuehrer

Doctor Helmut Katscher. Director Doctor Erich
Rudiger and Administrator Fraulein Lisa Mootz.

(LISA *catches up on the typewriter.* KATSCHER
turns to OSKAR, *waiting. He puts his cap on.*)

KATSCHER   As a member of the Reich's committee acting
under the authority of the Reich's Physician
and in the presence of the Director of the
Institute who in the absence of further
personnel and in full accord with policy shall
act in accepted lieu of a lawyer, I declare us
quorate and authorised to act as temporary
genetic health court for the Andernach district.

LISA   Quorate . . . Temporary . . .

(KATSCHER *falls silent allowing* LISA *time to
catch up. She finishes her typing.*)

LISA   Apologies.

KATSCHER   When I raise my hand like so you will stop the
record when I lower it again you will continue –
is that clear?

LISA   Yes. Doctor Katscher.

KATSCHER   Begin . . . I have been instructed by Reich's
General Himmler to ensure the special handling
of the human ballast in this region.

(*A silence.* KATSCHER *checks* LISA'S *typing.*)

KATSCHER   How many patients – (*Intimating* OSKAR.)
exactly – do you currently have on the wards
doctor Rudiger?

ERICH   How many do you need?

KATSCHER   I asked how many you have.

ERICH   Five hereditaries and two lunatics.

KATSCHER   I have express orders to ensure seven people
             are transferred to the Hadamar Institute.

ERICH   Why seven?

KATSCHER   I need seven. There is capacity for seven.
             Seven will go.

ERICH   Very exact.

KATSCHER   Precision is key.

ERICH   Good for you.

KATSCHER   So. Seven people will be transferred.

ERICH   All of the patients.

KATSCHER   Seven will go.

ERICH   It will shut us down.

KATSCHER   I offered you a job.

             (KATSCHER *raises his hand for* LISA *to stop
             typing.*)

KATSCHER   Lets keep it concise. Erase from here to here.
             Scrub it out. With pencil. That's it.

             (KATSCHER *points at the paper and keeps his
             hand over the keyboard.*)

ERICH   Why bother with this rigmarole if your mind is
             made up? Choose your seven and have done.

KATSCHER   Procedure must be followed. Records must be
             kept. We are not animals. It must all be above
             board.

             (KATSCHER *lowers his hand again.*)

KATSCHER   A plus or a minus for each one. Plus equals
             retain. Minus equals transfer to the Hadamar

for processing. Yes? A formality. Let's get on
with it. Which is first – Erich – which is first.

(ERICH *finds file.*)

ERICH   Anna Zollenkopf. Forty-two. She has lived
here since she was three years old.

KATSCHER   Patient number PF-4503.

(KATSCHER *raises his hand and* LISA *stops
typing.*)

ERICH   She's made good progress. She can walk
unaided. Nurse Clara taught her to sew. She
knows people in the village. They like her. She
shops for us. She communicates well and has
good relationships with other . . . She can . . .
She's done well. She's . . .

KATSCHER   What's the condition?

ERICH   Hydrocephalic idiocy. Aphasia and absences.
An exceptionally broad palate means some
speech difficulty. Petit-mal epilepsy and
episodes of melancholia.

KATSCHER   (*looking at her file*) She won't be competing in
the Olympics any day soon, will she?

ERICH   She's not the worst, she . . .

KATSCHER   Or winning a beauty contest.

ERICH   No.

KATSCHER   Christ's sake, she's a minus if ever I saw one.
A minus (*To* LISA.) note it.

ERICH   Why?

KATSCHER   A complete lack of faculty or the ability
to form judgements or recognise concepts.

ERICH   I'm not sure that –

KATSCHER   You know the criteria, Erich.

ERICH   But she can –

KATSCHER   Give her a minus and let's move on.

ERICH   Minus.

KATSCHER   Good.

                 (KATSCHER *throws the file to* OSKAR *to hold.*
                 KATSCHER *lowers his hand to* LISA *to start
                 typing. He picks up the next file.*)

KATSCHER   Patient DB-7392. A minus.

                 (KATSCHER *opens the file and shows it to* ERICH.
                 ERICH *thinks about objecting but changes his
                 mind.*)

ERICH   Minus.

KATSCHER   Selection confirmed. (*Picking up another file.*)
                 Next. Gerhard Wein. Twenty-three years old.
                 A syphilitic imbecile.

ERICH   Patient SK-2395.

KATSCHER   Doubly incontinent. A minus.

ERICH   Minus.

                 (KATSCHER *throws the file to* OSKAR. *He picks
                 up another.*)

KATSCHER   Selection confirmed. Next.

ERICH   Kurt Kremer. Eighteen years old. Less than one
                 metre tall. He's short. Disadvantaged, yes. But
                 in essence he's . . . short.

KATSCHER   Patient GF-0075. Ah . . . He has an IQ of only
                seventy. Minus.

ERICH   A minus.

                (KATSCHER *throws the file to* OSKAR. *He picks
                up another.*)

KATSCHER   Selection confirmed. Next.

ERICH   Margarete Hoven. Fifty-three. Often she is in
                good health. It depends on . . .

KATSCHER   Let's dispense with the sentimentals. Number,
                age and condition, that's all we need.

ERICH   LM-4938. Confusional insanity. Minus.

KATSCHER   Minus. Selection confirmed.

ERICH   Patient PT-4182. Indeterminate incapacity.
                Minus.

KATSCHER   Yes yes, selection confirmed. How many is
                that, Fraulein Mootz?

                (LISA *counts.*)

LISA   Six.

KATSCHER   Speak up.

LISA   Six.

ERICH   Get on with it. You know there is only one file
                left. Oskar's.

                (ERICH *throws file on the floor.* KATSCHER
                throws another on top of it.)

KATSCHER   No. There are two.

                (KATSCHER *throws his cap to* OSKAR *and
                loosens his jacket.*)

KATSCHER   There is something about the air up here. I
               could eat a horse. Small wonder you are so
               such a dumpling, Erich. Oskar – get me some
               of that pie. And some schnapps.

               (OSKAR *moves to find* FRAU POPPENDICK'S *pie
               behind desk and picks up a bottle. He brings
               them to* KATSCHER *who eats. He offers the plate
               to* ERICH.)

KATSCHER   Come. Keep your strength up. Fraulein Mootz.

               (*Both refuse.* KATSCHER *eats and drinks
               schnapps. A silence.* KATSCHER *belches.* OSKAR
               returns to his chair.)

KATSCHER   That's better. On the record . . .
               Hauptsturmfuehrer Katscher, on examination of
               the institute's staff records, discovered certain
               discrepancies and anomalies in the
               documentation appertaining to the employment
               of Fraulein Mootz, Administrator.

ERICH   Helmut, there's no need to . . .

KATSCHER   (*to* LISA *who has stopped typing, waiting for
               her to catch up*) Keep going . . . appertaining
               to . . . That's right . . . Are you ready?

               (LISA *nods.*)

KATSCHER   Fraulein Mootz has indeed been employed at
               the hospital since the summer of 1937.
               However it would seem her appointment was
               not externally advertised and had in fact been
               made from inside the hospital.

               (KATSCHER *waits for* LISA *to catch up.*)

KATSCHER   Not from within the hospitals staff but from
               within the patient body. Fraulein Mootz was
               admitted to the institute in 1936. She was
               picked up in the street by public ambulance

after making a disorderly and un-German
display. On arrival at the hospital she was
diagnosed with a psychotic breakdown. Once
admitted it became clear that Fraulein Mootz
was unstable, depressive and prone to periods
of intense self pre-occupation and that she was
suffering from an incurable nervous condition.

(KATSCHER *watches* LISA *type.*)

KATSCHER   She was therefore sterilised in the spring of
1937 as a sub-human.

(LISA *stops typing.*)

KATSCHER   I need one more patient to transfer to the
Hadamar. Yes? And two candidates. (*Looking
at the file.*) TP-9337. Thirty four years old.
Downs Syndrome. (*To* OSKAR.) Oskar – stay
there. (*To* LISA.) And you. Here. (*To* ERICH.)
You spoke to me of value – who do you value
more?

(OSKAR *and* LISA *stand in front of* KATSCHER.)

ERICH   No. I can't do that.

KATSCHER   Criteria. Criteria. Can you form a judgement?

LISA   Of course. Yes.

OSKAR   Yes.

ERICH   He knows what he likes.

KATSCHER   Shut up. Based on evidence will this hospital
remain open or will it be closed?

LISA   It'll be closed.

OSKAR   Closed.

KATSCHER   Do you know the difference between right and
wrong? Between a lie and a truth?

LISA — Yes.

OSKAR — Yes.

KATSCHER — You can act as a reliable witness to a crime?

LISA — Yes.

OSKAR — Yes.

KATSCHER — Save a baby from peril? Raise an alarm? 'Help, help come quick'?

LISA — Of course, I . . .

OSKAR — Help help.

KATSCHER — So which one, Erich? What will you do?

ERICH — No.

KATSCHER — (*to* LISA) You. Sit. Make a record. I'll do it for you then. As always.

(LISA *returns to the typewriter.*)

KATSCHER — It rests on the ability then to make a reasoned choice. I'm aware that Fraulein Mootz has this ability. She chose not to let me fall upon her because she is infertile and therefore the act would have been redundant. Yes?

LISA — Yes.

KATSCHER — So it all lies with him, Erich. Your court jester. Your fool. Let's have him decide.

(*A silence.*)

KATSCHER — Oskar. My friend. I have a duty. I follow orders. You understand? My orders are to send seven people to the Hadamar Institute. Six have been chosen. One more must go.

There's a choice. Between two people. One
person will stay and one person will go. The
choice is between you – let's call you the idiot
– and her – lets call her the whore . . . Who will
it be? That's the choice . . . The idiot or the
whore?

(*A silence.*)

ERICH   Oskar?

KATSCHER   The idiot or the whore?

(*A silence.*)

OSKAR   The idiot.

ERICH   What?

LISA   Oskar.

OSKAR   The Idiot. Idiot. Idiot.

(KATSCHER *laughs.*)

KATSCHER   No reasonable person would condemn
themselves. The decision is made. Minus.
Selection confirmed.

(KATSCHER *takes off his cap and loosens his
jacket.* LISA, OSKAR *and* ERICH *are motionless.*
KATSCHER *rips the record out of the typewriter
and puts it in his pocket.*)

KATSCHER   I'll complete the necessary paperwork. The van
will come for the selected patients next week. I
suggest Fraulein Mootz returns to her rightful
place on the ward. Look at it out there. It's a
beautiful day. A fresh start, eh Erich?
Everything clean and white and pure. What do
you say? One more try before I go? One last
challenge?

ERICH   You won't beat six seconds.

KATSCHER   I'll always beat you. Always.

                  (KATSCHER *exits*. LISA *moves to* OSKAR. ERICH
                  slams at his desk and kills his plants.)

Scene Two

On the surface of the ice.

A splash. KATSCHER *swims under the surface.*

OSKAR *counts and keeps counting as the shape disappears.*
OSKAR *counts to thirty and beyond. Blackout.*

Scene Three

On the surface of the ice/office.

OSKAR, LISA *and* ERICH *look at* KATSCHER *as he lies on the ice
frozen with twisted limbs. Blackout.*

Scene Four

On the surface of the ice/office.

LISA *and* OSKAR *look at* KATSCHER *and* ERICH *intertwined as
they lie together frozen with twisted limbs. Blackout.*

Scene Five

On the surface of the ice/office.

OSKAR *looks at* LISA, KATSCHER *and* ERICH *intertwined as they
lie together frozen with twisted limbs. Blackout.*

Scene Six

On the surface of the ice/office.

OSKAR *looks at* LISA, KATSCHER, ERICH *and* FRAU POPPENDICK *as they lie together with twisted limbs. Blackout.*

Scene Seven

On the surface of the ice/office.

OSKAR, ERICH, LISA, KATSCHER *and* FRAU POPPENDICK *lie frozen, dead, on the ice.*

BLACKOUT.